BY THE AUTHOR OF *A BOOK OF THOUGHTS THROUGH THE YEARS*

BIRDILYN (BLOSSOM) WATSON

VICTORY: MAKING IT THROUGH DIFFICULT TIMES

A COLLECTION OF
NOTES and REMEMBERANCES

A wholly owned subsidary of TBN

Notes and Remembrances: Victory in Difficult Times

Trilogy Christian Publishers A Wholly Owned Subsidary of Trinity Broadcasting Network

2442 Michelle Drive Tustin, CA 92780

Library of Congress Cataloging-in-Publication Data is available.

ISBN: 978-1-64773-878-5
E-ISBN: 978-1-64773-879-2

Dedication

This book is dedicated to my daughters—Ine, Caroline and Paulina—and to my supporters and friends—Rev. Dannie Mae James Green and Rev. Pamela Cole.

NOTES

ACKNOWLEDGMENTS

First, I must give honor to God, who is the creator and protector of my life. Through it all, He has kept me. There were times I did not even have enough sense to call upon Him, but I later learnt that He was present. Today, I continue to repeat the Psalm of David, "If the Lord had not been on my side....My help is in the name of the Lord, the Maker of heaven and earth" (Psalm 124:1, 8, NKJV).

To my mama, Mrs. Myrtle May Francis Watson, who departed this world too soon and who apart from carrying me for nine months, has left an indelible mark upon my life, I love you; I miss you and know that one day we will be together again. I still chuckle to myself about some of our private jokes and observations that you and I used to share. I must confess that I often regret the day I left you behind in the sun, because I thought you were not walking fast enough. I did not realize the changes that you had experienced.

To my papa, Mr. Luther William Watson, who labored in love for us, through rain and sunshine to provide all our needs. You were successful. If I had not known you, I would have to agree with some of my female friends when they say, "All men are no good." You provided that bridge between good and bad, responsible and irresponsible men.

My grandmother, midwife, and disciplinarian, Meme, Mabel Morgan MacDonald, I thank you, I thank you, I thank you. You are the only grandparent I knew and every day I wish that my children had the opportunity to know you.

To my beloved sister, Sister Del, Dolores Watson Robinson, who saw something in me that I did not and could not have known and decided to take me under her wings and train me to be something

5

better. As I write this line, tears are flowing. You should be here right now. You should be here right now!

To the family Sister Del worked for as a domestic, the Forbes family, thank you for accepting me. I do not know where you are now, but that does not eliminate my gratitude to you for the good things you showed me and how you tried to include me in your family: Mr. Forbes giving me ride to school; Mrs. Forbes teaching me ballet, etc. etc.

Honor, acknowledgment and respect to my children who have seen me go-through: Greg and Melissa and Ine, Augustine and Rose, Caroline, Charles and Catherine, Martinson and Eva, George and Ruke, Pius and Lisa, Dafe and Micheline, Paulina and Sam, Peter and Lilly. My prayer is that none of them will have to face the difficulties I faced, but if they do, they will be strengthened and never lose hope.

To the members of Bethel African Methodist Episcopal Church, New Bedford, Massachusetts and the members of the New England Annual Conference. You are my family. I have a little plaque on my wall that reads, "Friends are the family you choose for yourself." Little do you know how much you mean to me. If you had neglected me, I might have gone to another church, but you nurtured me into wellness and Christ-ness.

I give honor to my brothers and sisters: Charles, Fred, Flora, Alvin, Roxy, Bernice and Bev and to the memory of those passed on: Delores, Jenny, Lynette, Jocelyn, Leslie, Ernest, and Lee. All my nieces and nephews, cousins, aunts and uncles, wish I knew you all. I would gather you to myself. God bless you and keep you. For those yet unborn, I am praying for you.

I cannot neglect the educators in my life: The first two out of my home were Teacher Gascoigne, Headmaster at Kings Government

School and Miss Read, my A grade teacher. You did a wonderfully awesome job.

My best friend, Maureen, whom I see maybe every ten years: you are the best. You accepted me just as I am, even when we met in elementary school.

I apologize if I have left any name unlisted. Believe me, you are still appreciated, accepted and loved.

TABLE OF CONTENTS

NOTES

FOREWORD

This book lets you in on some real-life experiences that will pique your interest. You will stay alert and awake because you will find yourself through the situations written within! I think it is a must read!

– Rev. Dannie Mae James Green, retired guidance counselor and ordained minister in the African Methodist Episcopal Church.

If you are a person who has sailed through life with success and happiness, this book may not be for you. But if you are like the rest of us struggling to stay afloat, it will warm your soul to read Birdilyn Watson's remembrances of her days as a young mother. Her heart-wrenching experiences with domestic violence and double discrimination as a woman and a West Indian may not be the same as yours. Yet whatever you have been confronted with in life, you and the author have the same challenge: making it through the difficult times. In her book, Ms. Watson describes the supports that buoyed her up: her faith, her mother and grandmother, her love for children as well as for God's creation. In reading Ms. Watson's personal reflections may you be encouraged to try new ways to find victory for yourself.

–Rev. Pamela J. Cole, the most senior ordained minister in the area and the State president of Church Women United.

NOTES

NOTES and REMEMBRANCES:
INTRODUCTION

Failure to remember will bring us back to where we were. Remembering provides a pathway. "Forgetting" forces us into slavery, sin and shame, failure and distress. God reminded the children of Israel where they were coming from and how they got to where they are. He delivered them from slavery and bondage. He fulfilled the promise to take them to a land flowing with milk and honey. Will I find myself in any of these unfortunate situations? But with God on my side, I will know how to deal with it better. Some of the old hymns like: "Just as I Am Without One Plea" by Charlotte Elliott helps. When I initially made those notes, where was I physically, mentally, spiritually and emotionally? In some places positive changes were made. In others, changes were delayed.

This book started with some lamentations because that is where I was at that time in 1976. There are some chapters suitable for a memoir which is likely to be included at a later date.

As I go through the pages of my notes, I am taken back to challenging times in my life-Notes going back forty years. As I contemplated the necessity or uselessness to today's world, I came across an article November/December AARP magazine about former Senator Ted Kennedy's new memoir, True Compass, is based on notes he wrote fifty years before. History is being produced. I am a survivor. In the same old magazine is an article on "The Secrets of Resilient People" by Beth Howard. In discovering this magazine it's as if it were written just for me at a time as this. This documentation is taking place January of 2018 from notes dated 1976.

Today, June 9, 2016, after watching Steve Harvey's show, I must come back and open up my writing pages and keep going. Every successful person must jump. I have been used, abused and mistreated. But I must overcome and jump. These notes and circumstances began forty years ago. As King David said in Psalm 18:29, "and by my God have I leaped over a wall."

My pledge to publish by the end of 2016 did not happen.

Today is November 25, 2017, and I have not published this piece of writing I am just editing for the first book. As I turn each page, each hour, each day, each week, each month, each year, new opportunities and challenges present themselves.

"Yea though I walk through the valley of the shadow of death, I will fear no evil. For thou art with me, thy rod and thy staff they comfort me" (Ps. 23:4, KJV).

What is difficult and challenging about writing? Capturing the thought or idea and retaining it. Unless it is captured it disappears as vapor. So, getting it on paper instantly is most important. Imprison it. Then it cannot escape. Lock it up.

These journal notes were done at a time or season in my life which could be called my youth. In 1976, I was only twenty-eight years old. The season of maturity had not even started physically, mentally, emotionally or spiritually.

Over the years I've taken the time to write down thoughts and ideas on paper with the final hope of producing a book or books.

It has been many years. I've kept them. I've aged. The notes moved right along with me. So here they are. Some are dated. Others are not.

Some are extended, some are short and sweet. Some are identified and others are not. Some are words of wisdom while others are random thoughts. Most are serious, others are funny. Most are happy, others are sad. There is something for everyone in it. They are for the young, the mature, ugly or beautiful, black or white. Whoever you are, you are sure to find yourself in these pages.

Some lines are in poetic forms and others are narrative, simple deep thoughts.

As I travailed through the pages, I am taken back to relive some happier times and some not so happy days and nights. I ask myself, what were you thinking? It's hard to think back that far to re-feel those moments. However, I am determined to revel in them. For better or for worse, they are mine.

9/19/2003 My writings span many years. I am determined to compile and publish them shortly. Shortly could be now, next year or next year. However, it will be done!

My first book, *A Book of Thoughts Through the Years*, was published in 2018.

God bless you and may you find some comfort hidden in these pages, something to which you can relate and claim as your own. From my heart to yours.

Notes

Chapter 1

THOSE WERE DARK DAYS

In my journal January 20, 1976, is recorded as another very dull, long and cold day: those days were dark. It was a very difficult period in my life. The challenges were great. At times it appeared that they would consume me. All I could do was cry out to the Lord.

Things were not getting better and on January 23, 1976, I wrote: Go to bed with death hanging over my head and woke up feeling the same way. Is that all there is? No. God forbid. I have always thought that there is a lot more and I know there is better because the Bible says so and I firmly believe the Bible. One day I will be able to know for sure whether or not it is so. Just breathe and cry? No. Not so. I have put one hundred percent into life, and I do not by any means expect the same percent in return, but I do expect portion of it. Lord, help me to go through this day the way in which you desire. I do not want to hate my husband. I do not now hate him. I know one thing for sure; I want to get out of his way. He has caused me too much grief and shame. I love my son, and nothing will make me ruin his life. If I find that my presence will ruin him, I will not hesitate to step aside. Maybe when he grows up, he will understand. Lord, I do not want him to experience any more violence and screaming and shouting right there in the home. On television it is ok but in real life, dear Lord, it is unbearable.

Right now, there are just a few things that I would like to accomplish in life if the Lord permits: get my mother and father a decent home and seeing as much as possible of my mother and father. Please Lord, help me to accomplish these or as close as possible to these. I know that I do not always or even get exactly what I pray for, but just in this one instance, give me the courage and ability to do these two things.

Work a miracle and let my brothers have nothing but love in their hearts for each other. Love! Love! Not an envious love. Not a cautious love, but true, sincere and never-ending love. In my family, Lord, that would help a great deal. Together we could move mountains with just love. Do not take my mother and father away from me now. I need them now more than when I was an infant.

I cherished each moment that showed signs of improvement. January 24, 1976 is particularly noted.

Today is a beautiful day. Gregory, my nine-year-old son, without being asked, is polishing the few pieces of furniture in the house. What a wonderful gesture? Overall, it seems like a roller coaster ride.

I had moved out of the family home and was staying with my uncle in law. He is unmarried. However, he had his nephew and his wife and two children staying with him. They were very kind and gracious to me.

Nonetheless, there comes a time when I felt I need to be independent. My uncle owned some property and I moved into one of the apartments which I rented from him. As soon as I moved and was feeling settled, problems started again with my husband. He did not expect me to move to my own place.

After all, we usually get back together, kiss and make up and wait for the next explosion. By moving into my own place, I am sending a different message and he did not like it. It did not take long for him to begin to show his displeasure.

Chapter 2

GOOD SAMARITANS ARE STILL ACTIVE

Is it a Good Samaritan, an angel or a nightmare? In the early morning of July 9, 1976, I was awakened by a rap on my back door. I had just moved into the apartment and I had no phone. I always slept with the radio on in those days just to keep in touch with the outside world. It had been just the night before we retired to bed that my nine-year-old son had expressed joy at being able to sleep in his own bed for the first time in almost six months. I was also overjoyed to know that I had been able to provide some kind of joy for my son after what seemed like perpetual failure. Failure, not monetary wise but in the sense that I had to be separated from a well-furnished home, from all the luxuries I had made myself become accustomed to over the past ten years. No husband, no home, I should also say, no hope. But there is hope for me. I realized that by giving my life to Christ completely and entirely a few months prior to July 9, 1976.

At the first rap, I moved a little in the bed. I figured I am not hearing correctly. Of course, there was another rap on the door. At this point I became fully awake and turned over in the bed. The rapping became more consistent. I got up, put on my bed slippers and went to the door. I said, "Who is it?" but there was no answer. I repeated my question. Finally, someone answered.

He said, "Birdie." I realized who it was, so I became frightened out of my wits.

I did not scream. I said, "Go away." But that did not work. Suddenly I heard the creaking of the door. He had started to put all his weight on the door. I felt certain that this old and wooden paneled door would not be able to bear all this weight much longer. I opened the front door, ran downstairs and started rapping on the first-floor neighbor's door. The neighbor was elderly and did not answer. By this time, I could really hear the creaking of that old door and the tearing sound of wood, just like the falling of a tree. I became frantic. I opened the outside front door. All this time, my poor son was in his room. I doubt very much that he would be sleeping through all this, but I know that God would protect him. This person wanted to hurt me, not him.

Just as I opened the outside front door, there appeared out of what seems to be nowhere a young man on a bicycle. He said to me, "What is wrong?"

I said, "Someone is tearing down my back door." Without hesitation, he said he would check. He got off his bicycle, put it aside, and walked by me and up the stairs. By this time, my ex-husband had broken right through the back door and I could hear his footsteps going through the house. Unfortunately, both he and the Good Samaritan met in the front room.

I heard the Good Samaritan say, "Who are you?" I heard my ex-husband say the same. Then I heard wrestling and feet moving around. This was the ultimate. I had not experienced this before. This was brand new. Just as I thought I had seen it all—all the embarrassment and hurts and fears and frights. I had been by my sister's side on an occasion when she and her boyfriend had a quarrel or fight. As a matter of fact, I had experienced once when living with her, seeing her wrestling with her boyfriend for a knife that he had tried to use on her. We finally got away from him by going out the window. I swore to myself that this could never happen to me. Not me. My sister had been accused of having other boyfriends. But me, I was not in that category. I never wanted to be in that category either. But here I was-in a worse situation than her. I was married and was also trying to live a decent life with my own child. Did I really deserve this kind of treatment? I was not a prostitute. I really thought I deserve better. Whatever I have, I worked my knuckles to the bones for them. Not that my sister deserved any less.

It is a frightening thing and through all this not one of my relatives showed up on the scene or ever wrote me a line except for my mother and sister and brother in Jamaica. I have a brother and sister in New York City. I tried to keep in touch with them. I called and I wrote. No answer. When I did call and got in touch, their only advice to me was to move to New York. To me New York City is a very repulsive place. No human being goes there and remains human. I chose to move away from that place. Why would I want to go back there?

Next thing I know I was running down the street fast as I could. It had been raining the previous night and I could feel the dampness on the sole of my feet. I had lost my slippers. I was in my night gown. It was four thirty in the morning. I was screaming, out of breath and tired. All lights in the neighborhood started going on one at a time. I kept praying someone please call the police. There was no one else in sight. No sooner did I lose my slippers that I felt hands closing in on me. I tried desperately to keep on running. I could scream no more. No breath was left. He grabbed me and held me by the skin in my midriff and pulled me towards him. I thought this had to be the end. Being so tired and breathless, I thought, 'Let it be soon.' I was only scared for my son, Gregory, at this point. I, myself, had been through so much. I noticed that his hand was bleeding. He said, "See what your man did to me." I said, "What are you talking about?" He said, "I caught you with your man." I tried to explain between breaths that I did not know the man. He screamed and cursed at the top of his lung. I kept saying in between breaths, "Help! Help!" One lady opened the top half of her window and said, "I called the police. They will be here soon." That did not help. Everything seemed like eternity. Nobody cared. There was no one else in sight but the Good Samaritan on his bicycle riding around. My ex-husband kept screaming profanities at him. He did not move. He stood there on his bicycle. I was dragged on to the porch, and up the stairs. Dragged! Because I refused to go willingly! I was dragged by any part of my body that he could grip on to. There were bruises all over my body. His bleeding finger had bloodied my night gown around the midriff. It hurt.

After what seemed like an eternity, the police arrived. By then, I swear I could have been murdered and buried. They walked in. He had me sitting on the bed that I had purchased next to him in the bedroom. By this time, he had ordered our son, who was reluctant to do so, to go to his own room and stay there. I could hear him crying. My ex-husband told the casual and relaxed policeman, "There is no problem." Then I, the one who was suffering all the pain and embarrassment told them that I had been separated from him and that it had already gone through the courts. They asked for papers to prove it. I showed it to them. They claim it was not enough and there was nothing they could do about what happened. All they claim they can do is order him off the premises. They did not even inform me that if I wanted to press further charges, I should go down to the Third District Court.

They just figured that I am black and separated so I had to be a hardened criminal. I was scared out of my wits. They went down the stairs with him and left me and my son standing there. Immediately, my son and I went outside, and I decided to go to his uncle's house which was about three blocks away. On the way down, we met the cops, and they claim that I should stay there because my ex-husband went home. I assured them that I knew him, and he did not go home. Shortly after the police car drove off, I saw his car go by. He was so drunk. Thank God he did not see us. We ran down the street. Certainly, he went straight to the apartment and it was when he did not find us there that he came to his uncle's house. There, he barged in and he started to relate to them how he had caught me with my man. I said not a word. His brother tried to calm him; his uncle tried, but it did not work. Finally, they started talking hard to him. His brother stood between us and he hit his brother then me on the left side of my head. I swayed back and forth for what seems like an eternity then leveled. The next thing I knew, I was going upstairs. Everything and everywhere was confusion. The frightening thing about it is that when trying to relate these incidences to people, they seem to get a certain amount of thrill from it. To the listener it is drama. If only they had to live it.

There are Good Samaritans still around. They are alive and well. Read the parable of the Good Samaritan in Luke 10:25-37. Praise be to God.

I thank God that domestic abuse issues are now handled differently by law enforcement and the judicial system. Women are protected after aggressive lobbying to the law makers. I volunteered with the local women center to provide counseling and protection to women who are in abusive relationship.

NOTES

Chapter 3

Why Me?

Sometimes, most of the time, when things do not work my way or when the unexpected arises, I am inclined to ask, "Why me?" It does not seem possible, but I ask myself this question not only when misfortune strikes, but also when fortunate incidences occur. I am inclined to think about it, but it is not so easy to think up good reasons as it is to think up negative ones. I can always think up something negative or undeserving that I had done easier than something good and rewarding. When Jesus wanted to wash Simon Peter's feet, Peter found it easy to say to the Lord, "you will never wash my feet" (John 13:8, NLT). He was sincere. The Lord does not choose us because of goodness we have done. Jesus ate at Simon's house. Simon was a leper whom Jesus had healed (Matt. 26:6-13). He also visited and ate at Zacchaeus' home (Luke 19:1-10).

Zacchaeus was a tax collector who had not been so nice to the people. In his job as a tax collector, he cheated many people. He became rich. But Zacchaeus realized his guilt and worthlessness through the power of love that Jesus enforced on him. Jesus did not have to say to Zacchaeus "you know you are a sinner; you have to make amend." The power of Jesus' love was enough. He could not change himself. It took God's grace and mercy. The goodness of Jesus was enough. These are situations that people at times cannot handle, e.g., their guilt. After being really nasty to someone, yet that someone is still so nice to them and still maintain their ground. Mary did not weep and say, "Why my son?" when Jesus was on the cross suffering. Jesus Himself did not say, "Why me?" Instead, He says, "Father, forgive them for they know not what they do" (Luke 23:34KJV). Therefore, how dare I ask that question? A sinner like me! A pity party will not work. Take a deep breath, suck it in and move on. Amen.

We like to use Job as the model of patience and enduring suffering without becoming bitter. However, Job did get hurt when his friends blamed him for his suffering. While he was lamenting, God did not lighten his burden. He did give him strength to endure. Until Job realized the workings of God, he was not able to work his way out of his problems. Then he realized that they were actually blessings. He was made stronger. He learnt to call upon God. We tend to lift up Job as the example of the perfect faithful burden bearer, but he did his share of complaining. Certainly, he did not curse God and die as his wife advised, he hung in there and because of his endurance to the end he was rewarded by God with double his possessions and all his children. He was credited with being the most righteous man in the East.

What appeals to us and the reason other people are able to relate to us is that there seems to be a personal link, relatedness, oneness, and familiarity about our collective experiences. I am sure that other people can feel something from the author's experience, but of course, it is different. It is viewed differently. The experience to the one who has never experienced the facts, is frightening or just plain sympathetic or they could store the information in their brain to be used defensively as needed. It pays to read a great deal. From reading I have found that I will sometimes see someone or overhear a conversation and immediately say to myself "I have seen or heard that before." We sometimes blame it on premonition or dreams, but it also happens through other things. I cannot really say, "Why me?" because people have been too nice to me.

Chapter 4
Women's Role:

The Role of Women in our Society:

With no intentions of regarding myself as a women's libber, I have been quietly thinking about the primary role women do play and are expected to play in our society. After giving the obvious roles first thought: motherhood, wife, housewife, church leader, chauffeur, and teacher at home and out, breadwinner, why can't she also be given the opportunity to make drastic political changes? If anyone can, it is a woman.

After all, the man who is intelligent enough to listen to his woman's voice and realize these changes, gets applauded and cheered on. While he is enjoying all this elation and excitement, does he recall the voice that gave him the right direction? For example, looking through the Standard Times, which is the local newspaper, I came across an article on the role women are playing in the war in Ireland. Now, if women can be so effective in running a nation, can't they be even more effective in rebuilding the same nation? Given the opportunity with no political ties, I feel they can do it. It is not fair that women should be tied down by their husbands, by society and by just a plain rule of thumb.

Just as a marriage can no longer survive after the wife decides to quit, so women have the strong hold on a nation. If all women decided not to have children, then who would fight future wars? If women want to be active in organizations outside the home or even if they want to work, they have to run the home and then do the organizational work. Men go to work and come home to cooked meals and neat house and clean clothing all waiting for them.

Women have always played significant roles in the Bible. Esther, Hagar, Hannah, Mary, Elizabeth, Ruth, Naomi e and many others, just to name a few. Queen Esther saved the Jewish nation when she learned that there was a plan to annihilate the Jewish nation living in Persia. She risked her own life by initiating an audience with the King. In so doing she knew that the King could have her killed. She sent a call to the Jewish community to have a three day fast. And Esther determined to save her people, especially after her uncle Mordecai reminded her that she too may perish and that she may have been queen for the purpose to top the annihilation plan and to save the nations.

Jesus, our Lord and Savior, came to us through the Blessed Virgin Mary. Hagar, Sarah's Egyptian maid gave birth to her husband, Abram's child, Ishmael. Hannah, who was considered barren, gave birth to Samuel, one of God's greatest prophet and judge. Elizabeth gave birth to John the Baptist in her old age. Ruth, through her faithfulness and devotion to her mother-in-law, Naomi, gave birth to Jesse, King David's father and is in Jesus' lineage.

Chapter 5
CHOOSING TO INTERACT: COMMUNICATION LINES

People are unpredictable. Do your own thing and it's offensive; do their thing and it is also offensive. Today is one of the days I am happy that I grew up with a large family. It is proof that one can choose to be happy or sad. It helps me to deal with the different personalities in the church, at work, and at home. I was brought up with the doctrine to respect and obey my elders, but it would appear to me that the older generation resent being respected. It makes them feel old. How can this generation survive when we are talked down to by our elders? The people who should be showing respect and love are demonstrating hatred and resentment.

Have you ever gotten the impression that someone is trying to speak to you but in actuality they are speaking at you? You reply to their address and they look right over your head and smile with the person behind you or next to you or in front of you. Sometimes it is done deliberately, sometimes not. When with a group, I try to study the people first before I can really feel at home and really and truly participate in whatever is going on. I prefer to be spoken to directly, and I don't like to have to lip read.

In so short a life span I have met so many different people. Just imagine the older people who have been around for ninety or one hundred years! I cannot even try to recall some of these people. One thing for sure ninety nine percent of the people I met have been nice. The people who have not been nice are the ones closest to me. I love people, but I hate prejudice and pretension. The worse thing about meeting an insincere person is that I can always know from the very first time he or she opens her mouth. Yet, I cannot help staying there and listening to them. Listen sincerely with the hope that their minds will change, and they will start acting sincerely. Hoping they may have a change of attitude and behavior. But most times though, as soon as I say something, they do realize that we are opposites and immediately we become friends.

Chapter 6

Genesis...1

NATURAL BEAUTY:

Why do we continually destroy all the natural beauty that God himself has created for us?

No painter can even combine colors or retrace the kind of art that God has outlined for his earthly beings. Just think or look at the art of one's life. No matter how dirty and evil and frustrated it seems to be there is always that little trace of beauty that is zigzagging its way in and out. The only thing is most times we fail to see the beauty since it is usually short lived, or maybe it is so beautiful that we regard it as unimportant. Remember the summers off from school as compared to the summers now we have to spend working. However, those days were necessary to prepare us for where we currently are. If we have become handicapped or disabled or limited, think of the days we were able to do all the things we are not able to do now and be grateful.

Life is a learned art. It attracts good and bad. It all depends on how it is interpreted. If we think that all incidences are or will be unfortunate, then it will appear to be so. We know that life is a learned art because of the different stages we are expected to go through. There are times when the tendency is to hate, and you, only you, the one tempted can avert that feeling or from acting in that manner. I can recall the day when I was so battered and torn by the people closest to me that I was tempted to hate my very own son (child). Now there was absolutely no beauty in my immediate surroundings to suggest otherwise, so I had to turn to my inner self for support and I prayed to God not from my lips, but from my heart. Slowly my feelings changed, and I found myself. From that experience I can now understand why some children grow up hating or why parents mistreat and abuse them. When I came to myself that day, fear was upon me. I had become afraid of my own self. I am praying to God that it will never, never happen again.

Chapter 7

The Beauty of Children

Jesus had his own view on children. Little children were being brought to him that he might touch them, but the disciples wanted to turn them away. And Jesus was very displeased and said to them, "Let the little children come to me, and do not forbid them; for of such is the kingdom of God" (Mark 10:14, NKJV).

CHILDREN AT PLAY:

"Children, Children, yes mama" is a call and response game we used to play as children in the rural areas in Jamaica. There was no television and barely a radio, so we made up our own games and modify the existing ones. So, on October 2, 1976, when I encountered these children at play, it brought me back to my childhood days.

It has been many, many years since I have heard such beautiful noises: The laughter and chatter of little voices. Such happy tunes can never be reproduced. It may live on many more years in the mind but never copied. Forty years later, at this time of writing, with the popularity of the video, face book, internet, tabs, etc., I must recant that statement. Anything can be reproduced. These are little ones moving all over, some of them seem to be no taller than 6 inches. They all are doing what makes them happy. Standing here watching these children, I am wondering if they realize that they will go this way only once, but why should they care, only the present matters. As if their own little voices were not music enough, they utilized whatever is closest to them to make a sound. It all blended as if perfected by an artist.

TEACHING CHILDREN:

You must become like a little child to enter the Kingdom of heaven (Mark 10:15).

Teaching children is one of the most difficult tasks I have ever attempted. It is not a regular class, but the same problems exist. When teaching, the first thing to understand is that all the children are different. Each one also has their rate and method of learning. The only thing about children is that if they are not interested in the subject matter, they show you right away. They will not tolerate anything they disregard. It is very disappointing to watch the reactions of children when you think you have worked up a beautiful and perfect idea, hoping that they will really enjoy it, only to see them stare at you with disgust or a big question sign on their little faces. Children are unpredictable. On the whole, I enjoy teaching them though. There are times when, overhearing a remark such as "I learned something today." I feel elated. Maybe, if we would learn to love them first, then work on further, the teaching would not be so difficult.

Chapter 8

DREAMS

Dreams are beautiful. They help you to fulfill in your sleep things you wish for while awake and conscious. Have you ever had such a beautiful dream that you hoped it was real life? Dreaming that you are just as free and happy as when you were a child or dreaming of being in some far- away place that you have hoped to be? It is human nature that when we have nice and beautiful dreams, we want to believe that they are true or will be fulfilled. The sad and ugly ones make us fearful and worried. They are called nightmares. Just as though the Lord is reading our little minds, he usually backs up the bad dreams with two or three very good ones.

God communicated with many of the prophets in the Old and New Testaments through dreams: Joseph, Daniel, Joseph, Mary's husband.

In Genesis 37:5, Joseph, next to youngest of twelve siblings, disclosed to them his most ostentatious dream that he had of being ruler over them and that even his mother and father would bow down to him. His siblings were angry with him and when the opportunity arose, they planned to get rid of him, at first to kill him, but then they decided to sell him into slavery in Egypt. Eventually his dream came true. Joseph became a ruler in Egypt. There was a period of famine throughout the land, and they went to Egypt seeking food. Joseph was second in command and they did not recognize him. But Joseph knew them. Should we make it a habit to disclose our dreams? How, when, and to whom should we disclose our dreams? How much weight do they carry in our real life? Joseph also accurately interpreted dreams for Pharaoh.

Daniel was a dreamer and an interpreter of dreams. This was his gift from God. And while in exile in Babylon he was summoned to the king's palace to interpret a dream (Daniel 4).

At least twice Joseph, Mary's husband received instructions from God in a dream (Matthew 1, 2).

And Pilot's wife complained of insomnia due to the way Jesus was being treated and advised her husband not to have anything to do with Jesus, "for I have suffered many things this day in a dream because of him" (Matthew 27:19, KJV).

I am not talking about people who are superstitious and live by their so-called dreams. These dreams become nothing but a form of witchcraft, pitting families against each other and neighbor against neighbor. God does not work like that. He offers peace, healing, and love.

Chapter 9

HAPPINESS AND MUSIC:

Happiness and music seem to go hand in hand. The tune as soon as it is sung or played it seems to disappear into the air. It is short-lived. Happiness seems to be just as short. We spend so much time trying to reach that climax and, in an instant, it passes from us. How can the wedding day be prolonged? Staying married? Reliving the moment? Many pictures are taken, but the moment is gone. It was snapped by the camera; however, it cannot be delayed. It must move on. We have no power to hold it back. Play that tune and once you lift your finger off the key and move on to the next. It is done. It is gone. It slipped away unapologetically. You cannot hold it back. King David introduced music in worship.

It was young David, the shepherd boy, who played the harp for King Saul when the evil spirit came upon him (2 Samuel 16:23). David would play and Saul's mood would change to happy and pleasant. Music makes you happy. It cheers you up. Did not King David dance out of his robe? It's hard to be still while the instruments are playing. You cannot remain sad when you hear the music.

NOTES

Chapter 10

Rain, Rain, Rain

Has anyone ever stopped to think of the necessity of rain? In some regions of the world, rain is only a humbug. But just imagine that in other regions it means life or death. This is the sequence of thoughts when we hear rain in the western region: umbrella, raincoat, wet, time, work or school, football or basketball games cancelled. Humbug!

In other regions, rain is glory, food, water, money, and life itself. See, these people whether it's rain or sunshine, they are still expected to fulfill their requirements for the day. What if we were to change our attitude just a little and think of the beautiful green trees or the rainbow when we hear the weatherman predicting rain? In the underdeveloped regions e.g., parts of Africa, there is no weatherman. They have to follow the signs of the time, cloudy sky or certain birds flying low in flocks or the pig dancing around, the rolling thunder.

If at times, we would give ourselves a little time to relax and enjoy the things that God has given us, we would be able to see the good points and enjoy them better. Which of us can send the rain? Which of us can stop the rain? Like Elijah prophesied in 1 Kings 17:1 and 18:41 that there would be no rain or dew for three and a half years. Just imagine, if we could stop or start the rain, it would be another commodity like the Arab oil embargo or the wheat for the Russians. It would be another reason to be friends or enemies with another country. Or just imagine if we had to go to a bank to borrow rain and the treasurer would decide whether or not to lend us depending on whether you were black or white, my job, the area of the community in which I live or according to my religion. As it is right now, in some regions the earth is parched, and everything becomes lifeless and people die off or they get so much rain that floods wash away and destroy all their belongings. We all try to understand why these things happen, but apparently this is one way that God can keep us humbled and show who is in control.

Chapter 11

Who Makes The Plant Grow?

Have you ever watched a plant grow from seed? About eight weeks ago I purchased two big beautiful avocados. After consuming all the delicious pulp, I decided to try to grow a tree. I plunged the avocado seed in a container with some warm water and placed it in an inconspicuous spot in the kitchen away from direct sunlight. Every day I peeped at it to see what was happening. It seems for weeks upon weeks nothing happened. I gave up but refused to throw it out. About one week went by, and then I decided to check if there were any changes and there were. I actually saw roots peeping from the center of the seed. I clapped my hands in joy.

Never give up on God! God makes the tree grow is true. He can do anything. Nothing is too hard for Him. And all things are possible with Him. All we have to do is plant and He will make it grow. He will supply all our needs according to his riches in glory (Philippians 4:19).

Notes

Chapter 12
Sites and Scenes:

Traveling from New Bedford, Massachusetts, to New York City in the early 1970s: One can see almost a whole world unfold in this short journey. The trip started out calmly, the highway not so crowded, only three lanes of traffic. Farther on, it becomes four lanes. Then you get into the heavy traffic through Fall River and into Providence. Suddenly, you are traveling in four and five lanes of heavy traffic for most of the way. At the start, you can see beautiful green trees or colorful fall trees around you. It was the fall season. Farther on, the buildings start to increase. They get into thicker and thicker cluster and they also get higher and higher. Finally, you get into the big city, New York and all around, everywhere, below and above, it's the noise, trains, cars hooting, lights, traffic lights, car lights, neon lights-is it day or night? Wall to wall people, buses, taxis; everybody seems to be doing a slow trot. There are children running from place to place. Some of the people are old and ragged looking. Some are so well dressed you want to think you are in Hollywood. Others are just "mad" or drunk looking. Others are walking solemnly in small family groups all dressed up. They seem to be on their way to church or coming from church. Where is the church? How does one know a church as distinguished from the other buildings?

Look at the sidewalks! Garbage piled sky high. The garbage bins are there, but I do not think anyone knows the use of them. The people are all speaking just as briskly as they are walking. Some are speaking English; some seem to be speaking Spanish. Others speak dialects of many different countries.

Experiencing New York City

Today, I am in New York City. I lived in the United States eight years and worked at different jobs, but this place always intrigued me, not enough for me to want to live here, but its complexities keep me thinking. Have you ever had the opportunity of seeing Wall Street at noon time? Winter, summer, spring or fall, it is the same. The only difference is that in the winter everyone seems to be smoking. At noon time, there are people all over. They are stumbling all over each other. There are black people, red people, white, Chinese, short, tall, fat, and skinny. They are all hurrying – to go where? The vendors with their carts are making change, collecting money, advertising their goods; the ice cream man is there too, the pizza is getting baked right there. Up the street there is a demonstration. The speaker climbs on the steps of the most conspicuous building and starts speaking. The crowd below is shouting their different lines everyone looks in that direction for a short while, have to get back to eating or making sure I keep my place in line or I have to get to the department store to get the dress – after all I have one hour in which to go through all these different experiences – it's lunch hour.

The speaker is discussing the Vietnam War and people seems to be drawing closer and closer to the demonstrators until you did not know who is who. This was in 1969. It was just one big mass of heads and bodies. The speaker now realizes he has quite an audience, so he speaks or shouts louder and louder and finally he says no more. He is silent. The crowd shouts and pants for more, but poor guy he is tired and thirsty. In another three hours it's as though this is a residential little district and not even the dogs are allowed to bark here until 5:00, 6:00, and 7:00 a.m. Then it's time to rush for the subway and O Rotten Gotham, an essay by Tom Wolfe, tells that much better than I could.

SITES AND SCENES:

WHAT DO YOU SEE?

People, garbage, dogs, cars and children
They are all calling for help
The people are running
They seem so tired
Some dirty, some clean
All going in the same direction
The children are entangled with the dogs
Children screaming, dogs barking
Children eating from paper bags on the street
Dogs picking up grub from sidewalk
The garbage laughs at you loud and clear
It sings a song as you get closer
The flies aim at your head
But the garbage just keeps on laughing
Guess where you are?
It could be anywhere in the world.

Notes

Chapter 13
HE CALLS, APPOINTS AND EQUIPS.

HOW GREAT IS OUR GOD?

(Exodus 31:1-11)

God is great.
God is wonderful.
Jesus performed many miracles during his lifetime here on earth and after his death and resurrection he still is performing millions more. When we look at the great wonders around us just think, the seasons change, in this same place I am today, only less than three months ago I had all the windows wide open in an effort to get cool, today I have all the windows closed and the heater turned on full blast trying to get warm. Scientist will try to give us a reasonable cause for the change in the weather, why rain falls but what they cannot tell us is where in the world the skies, moon, sun and stars come from. They have to guess their beginnings.

What's more? God gave the order to build the tabernacle and he provided all the resources. He named the people with the gifts and talents needed to complete the tasks. God will not call and appoint to do that which he will not provide support. He is detailed and specific. Moses was given instructions to build the tabernacle.

This brief paragraph in Exodus 31:1-11 provides us with the care God has for us. He has every detail about us. He knows what is to be done, how, by whom and when. Just in case you do not know who Bezalel is, He says "he is the son of Uri, the son of Hur, of the tribe of Judah." You cannot make a mistake. God told Moses, "I have filled him with the spirit of God, in wisdom, in understanding, in knowledge, and in the manner of workmanship, to design artistic works, to work in gold, in silver, in bronze, in cutting jewels for setting, in carving wood, and to work in all manner of workmanship" (Exodus 31:3-5, NKJV).

Don't get in God's way when he makes an appointment. You may not think much of the individual, but God thinks enough of him/her to fill them with the Holy Spirit. Humble yourself and submit to God's calling.1 Corinthians 12:4-5 states, "There are diversities of gifts, but the same spirit. There are differences of ministries, but the same Lord." So, let us respect each other's gifts and calling.

Chapter 14
Ups And Downs

The ups and downs of our lives are comparable to the wiggly ups and downs the worm makes, only that the worm's is visibly and physically so since it does not have a mind. It does not have enough sense to try and disguise it. We stand upright and look straight ahead while our minds are far away. The Bible tells us that God gave dominion over all living creature, great and small to us (Gen. 1:26). Yet so many of the living creatures are larger than human beings. Job speaks of Leviathan, the great sea monster that everyone feared. Male and female humans were the only creation in God's image and are accountable to him.

We have what the psychologists call mood swings. Sometimes we are happy, other times we are sad. We swing from depressed to super excited moods. As we swing back and forth there is the need or balance. So that we are not stuck in one place in one mood, our emotions help us change as needed or essential. Our senses of sight, hearing, feeling, taste speech keep us in tow. Should we cry when everyone else is laughing is a sign that we are out of the realty one.

Walking is one of the most relaxing and satisfying activity I know. It is like medicine to both body and mind. As I walk along the street, I sometimes wonder what would become of me if I did not have these two beautiful feet that God gave me. I walk down the street and I can see people hurrying, eating, drinking, and some are happy, some are sad. The ones I like most are the little children in groups. They are usually laughing. They seem to be so happy. They have no care in the world. And that brings me back to my carefree days frolicking in the rain to school or to the shop or going to visit my grandmother.

NOTES

Chapter 15

AUTOMOBILES: THEN AND NOW

Cars are one of the most expensive, most unreliable commodities there is on the market. They cost more than some homes (at the time of this writing), or just as much as purchasing a home, but yet there is very little return on these things. It is not fair to the consumer that after making a loan for nearly six thousand dollars, that as soon as he drives the (six thousand dollars) piece of goods one blocks over fifteen hundred dollars is lost right then and there. The price of cars keeps climbing, but people keep buying them, so now just so everyone gets their piece of the rock, the insurance keeps skyrocketing too. The price of gas is out of reach. Repairs, no one will even take a quick look at the car without charging twelve to fifteen dollars. In an effort to counteract the high cost or in an effort to help consumers, writers have started publishing books telling people how to repair their cars, of course, this means you have to sit down and read one paragraph for days when something goes wrong while the car sits there.

If you are impatient, you will take the book to the car and try to repair it while following the directions only to find that it still doesn't work. Now, the book does not tell you how to retrace your steps. So, there you are, the car in a worse mess than before. The mechanic will be charging double because he figures you had been trying to cross him in his trade. If I had to start life over from childhood, I would, not give up my pony and wild, wild country. No, sir! That is too much freedom to give away. Freedom, that once we have made ourselves slaves to the modern way, we cannot untie those chains and return to them.

This was written in 1976. Those costs mentioned have now in 2014, gone through the roof. Gas cost less than one dollar per gallon then compared to four to five dollars in some places today. Homes can cost anything, up to millions and cars are up to ten times more than the six thousand mentioned. Looking at those figures, one would say, "What were they complaining about?" However, wages were much lower also. Praise be to God; I have lived long enough to experience change and be able to look back and see the balance in my thoughts then and now.

Chapter 16

WHAT DOES IT MEAN TO BE?

While visiting my parents in Jamaica in early 1976, I was somewhat depressed. The only thing I think that could soothe my worried mind was to take a long, long walk or to sit by the seaside alone. I did not want to know anyone. I wanted to pass through the crowd unnoticed. I went to another town twenty miles from home on the bus. On the way back, I decided to get off by the beach. I did, and I sat there and watched all these happy people splashing in the water. I suddenly grew up. I realized that happiness does not mean a big beautiful home. It does not mean the best cars. Nothing that we possess can make us happy. I realized that happiness is a frame of mind. Here I was, sitting alone, I had almost everything, or things that would make most of these people envy me. But they are the ones who were happy. I know for a fact that some of them had to go home and share their rooms with four or five other persons. They did not know what it is to own a car or a home, or even to have a husband although they have several children. Some of them don't know what it is to have three pairs of shoes. Yet, they were happy, even if it were for those brief moments.

I am documenting this journal in 2015 and would assuredly say, ditto, to those sentiments. It has not changed.

It is impossible to know other people unless you know yourself. Etiquette begins in the home, so does most other things.

Things do not make you. You make things.

NOTES

Chapter 17

DISCOVERING GOD

"A broken and contrite heart O God, thou wilt not despise" (Psalm 51:17, KJV).

More and more I learn that God is my only source of strength and courage. He has healed my broken heart many times. He has healed my wounds. He has always given me the chance to start new. If I can remember well, He always has, ever since I had enough sense to say, "Mama." I could always feel the presence of God. I am convinced of this because from reading the Bible and some of the revelations in my life I know God was always walking by my side. He is real. I am the one who turns away from him because I did not believe that he could be really so concerned about me. Thank God, one day I came to my senses. I am getting closer to Him, and I have given Him full control of my life. His will is my will.

NOTES

Chapter 18

JUMP TO CONCLUSION

Following a negative incidence at church on February 21, 1977, I wrote:

What was said that night after choir rehearsal just served to strengthen the negative notion about people who are separated, divorced or in the process of divorce: that they are classified as men chasers? This was backed up even in the pastoral prayer that people should try to love each other without emotion. How can anyone love without emotion? When I do love, it is the type of love that involves emotion. I am not so naïve as to think that a young pastor would want a cast off left over, especially with a child. I am not so stupid. If I look at him mad, it's for a different reason. I am working for the Lord, and I want to continue to work only for the Lord. What kind of concern was it he had for me? I don't see it. It is nothing more than pure curiosity. If I were to fall in love, one thing for sure, I think I deserve more. I am not about to make the same mistake again. How can someone be in love with a person they don't even really know? I am not even thinking of remarrying because I love my independence so much. I go to sleep when I want. I clean the house when I feel like it. If I don't feel like washing or ironing clothes, I don't. But I cannot help feeling a little upset because this is the second time that this has happened to me.

There is only one person aside from God who understands me and that is my mother. She knows and understands me. If I should lose her now, I don't know what I would do. Sometimes I feel so alone for a human friend, a real human friend who will sit and listen to me for a while without showing sympathy or making judgment. People who know me will not think that I am looking for someone.

My God I need it someone who understands! But I will depend on God. Most times it is my hands that become slippery and let go of His strong and mighty palm. Whenever I dusted myself off and get up again, that arm is still there ready to pull me up and to my feet again. Thank God.

Chapter 19

TODAY:

What is today? Where is today? Who is today? Date, time, place?

Today is full of joy and disappointments. I give them all up to God. He can handle both alike. Me, I cannot handle either. The Lord giveth and the Lord taketh, so says Job in his justification of God's righteousness. Just give yourself and everything back to the Master. With His powerful and mighty arms, He will lift us up and put us on our way again. More and more the Lord speaks to me. He strengthens me, guides, protects and keeps me.

He will do the same for you.

Notes

Chapter 20

What About Me?

If my eyes should close tonight
If tomorrow never comes
For me, I want everyone to know that life has been full.
My cup runneth over
I have a few regrets but less than most people in my age group and with the same background.
My life has been lived so fast that if it should be taken early, it would be a surprise to everyone except me.
I have loved and been loved. I have given birth. I, myself, I have been born twice.
I have learnt to take life day by day and thank God for even the ones he did not allow me to see.
Most of my real dreams have been crushed. I have hopes to see them through as far as possible.

NOTES

Chapter 21

Hungering And Thirsting:

Hungry and thirsty,
Their soul fainted in them.
Then they cried out to the Lord in their trouble,
And He delivered them out of their distresses.
Psalms 107:5-6 (NKJV)

There are times when I feel as completely helpless, fruitless and worthless, that if I had not realized the goodness of the Lord, I could wander or go astray. Nothing can satisfy my hungry soul but the Word of God. It soothes my broken heart. Instead of crying tears of sorrow, I cry tears of joy. I can see goodness in the worse. There always seem to be a brighter tomorrow even in snow and rain and most of all in the storms of life. I can see hope in the garbage and on the most desperate looking faces. In between those hopes and the brighter tomorrow are the things that roll the chariot, troubles, trials, tears and sorrows, laughter and joy. I get lonely at times even in a crowd of ten or fifteen people. Many times, when I get so lonesome, I reflect on home: my mother and father, brothers and sisters, and most of all, Colter, my birthplace in Jamaica.

I still have not found words fit enough to express my feelings during those happy far-out days. May God grant everyone at one time or other some of those glorious experiences? O Lord, please let there be more love in the world. Let love flow throughout the land, the land you promised Abraham, Isaac and Jacob, that their children will be like the sand on the seashore. Where are these children? Who are they? Sometimes I look at my own son and wonder if he really is a part of me. I pass my neighbor on the street and not a word to him. He is my brother/sister, may we always be reminded of that. I shall always remember my people and I still want to be a part of them. Let the Lord's will be done.

Chapter 22

My *child*, my first born, Greg.

I have watched him grow from the cradle on. What is more exciting, he continues to grow, physically and mentally. I can still feel and see the difference in growth just as though he were still in my womb. Sometimes I stand by his bedside and watch him sleep—so innocent and peaceful. It is at this time that I feel the most sorrow for him, because I know what he will have to face later. It is then that I feel so helpless that I say, "Lord, take him. He is all yours."

As I write this paragraph in 2018, I declare that Greg is a married man with three girls. Greg completed high school, spent some time in the National Guards, worked at different jobs and currently works for one of the national cable company. He started college but did not finish. He still loves to read.

He is a loving husband and father and is involved in the life of his children. I appreciate that he is different from his father. He is kind and mature.

NOTES

Chapter 23

MAKING THE WRONG ASSUMPTIONS

Sometimes, even I, make the miserable mistake of thinking life is easy and that it is easy to get anything one wants in life and then start looking around myself and my family. I do not need to look far to realize that it is not so. I am sitting here and the only person whom I can see appearing and reappearing is the agonized face of my mother. I can recall the same look that was on my grandmother's face a few years before she died-toothless, old and worried. I did not attend her funeral because I was in the city in school. I did not realize how much she meant to me then. I was not her favorite grandchild and was only twelve at the time of her death. Today, at the age of twenty-eight (1976) almost twenty-nine, having one child of my own to bring up alone, almost divorced, having suffered all the downfalls of life, the thing money can buy, almost all taken away from me. I can recall those looks on her face, the tone of her voice and even the manner in which she walked and say almost exactly why, when and what she is doing or thinking. My grandmother brought up her children alone. They all suffered hunger pain together. They all worked the fields together. There were times when they all slept on the floor together. They all walked miles to fetch water together.

Today, I am faced with the same problem but in a different society, because these are what we call modern times. Do richer and more prosperous times make the burden any lighter or the tears any saltier or fresher? I would say no. when I started writing I was not thinking of myself or my grandmother, I had in my mind uppermost my mother.

When last I saw her in 1976, she seemed to be carrying the same agony and burdens around just as my grandmother did. She had that worried look on her face. As a matter of fact, she needed new denture just like my grandmother. Need to break that chain! She is suffering from high blood pressure and diabetes. One stroke and a major surgery had already limited her. Oh my God, she had the same unfulfilled dreams as my grandmother. It was shocking to hear a few days that she was hospitalized for a cyst in her breast. I remember the last time I saw my grandmother her right breast was so hard you could not tell if she had a rock hidden in her bosom. With nine children, all of whom grew up too fast; the family is completely broken down, nothing up. We could be a large rich family, but the devil is always there, grabbing ahold of us. Because everyone grew up so fast, none can help the other. Sometimes I wish we were all children together again, just as we could learn all over how to be nice to each other in a sincere manner. My mother, her unfulfilled dreams of her children building her a beautiful home – my, God knows she deserves it more than any other mother in the world. I just wish I could do for her even half the things I want to do. I do not want her to die frustrated and broken down. I want to see her die happy – not only in the Lord, but in us. I keep hoping that the Lord will provide a way for me to do this either before she dies or before I die. I do not want to cry at her funeral if she goes before me because I want to be sure that she dies happily and happy. I just wish I could bring back that smile on her face again. All I can see ahead of me are some of those frustrations coming towards me. Will it be any easier? No. But I only have to pray to the Lord to give me the strength to bear it all. I also hope that from observing my grandmother and mother that I have learnt something also. I hope one day I will be able to draw a picture of Meme's solemn face – if I sit long enough to contemplate, I shall make it.

Chapter 24

DEDICATED TO MY GRANDMOTHER, MEME

I miss you, Meme
No other Johnny cakes
Can taste like yours!
No other cartwheel dumpling like yours

Our hairs have not been oiled
The oil nuts have all fallen
To the ground and rotted.

The coconut trees have all
Almost been diseased and dead
Coconut oil is a thing of the past
That sweet savory custard, no more!

I still tease Flora and Bugsy
About you
They were your favorites.

The days with Nicey, our first cousin, are still remembered
I used to read the psalm for you
I remember some of the songs you used to sing too
Others I am still trying to sing.

When I reflect on the good and the bad times together, it is as though
you were there only yesterday, or you left this morning to go to church.
Mama Beck is calling you. She is ready to start the journey.
One horrible thing though, I can remember the month in which you
died, but not the month in which you were born.
Blue Hole is still there. I do not go by there half as many times as I

need to, but I know it is there. As a matter of fact, I have not gone by there in the last ten years.

The naseberry tree is there. I love you.

Chapter 25

INNER VERSES OUTER BEAUTY

"I beseech you therefore, brethren, by the mercies of God, that you present your bodies a living sacrifice, holy, acceptable to God which is your reasonable service" (Romans 12:1, NKJV).

We are all dressed up as pretty as we think. Just as we prepare our outward appearance to be so beautiful, we spend hours on just one part, namely, the hair, which takes from three to six or more hours at one time. Yet our souls which take no time at all from us, we disregard it. The soul is the ultimate body, and this is what should be cared for so tenderly and lovingly. If we should try to justify spending all those hours on one particular portion of the body, then where are we left when God says, "Your bodies are the living temples of God" (Rom. 12:1)? Not just certain parts, but the entire body.

Where do we get off thinking and acting like we are better than some other people? God made all of us, including his only Son in the image and likeness of Himself. To some he gives more beauty, others more wisdom, others more hair, different complexion. Yet instead of using what He has bestowed upon us for the betterment of other people and His kingdom, we blow ourselves up as though we are our own creator and that we are all those things because we are so good. We should remind ourselves that God has all the power in His hand. He giveth and he taketh (Job 1:20). We are nothing. We are powerless. As soon as we think we are so powerful, see how quickly everything crumbles at our own feet. We had all that wisdom, and we don't even know where we have gone wrong. It is just like Peter. He was doing fine walking on the water as long as he kept his eyes on Jesus. The moment he looked away, he started sinking (Matt. 14:30). Let us not look away but take a grip and never let go.

NOTES

Chapter 26

Let us Hear from the Children

We are one in the Lord. It is so wonderful when we know that Jesus loves us. When we can look at a flowering plant in spring and see God's wonder at work or look at the tree that to us was lifeless in the winter and now it is showing all the vital signs of life. It is in the same manner we live to die and die to live again. God is powerful. He works wonders.

Just imagine after all that Jesus had done in front of all those people, he healed the sick, raised the dead, set at liberty those that were in bondage; he set the prisoners free; forgave sins and these same people crucified him. They spat upon him. They put nails through his hands and his feet. They appreciated his miracles and his goodness, but what they could not withstand was the laws he challenged and tried to correct. To tell them to love their enemies and do good to those who hate them, turn the other cheek, and to love their neighbors as they love themselves, were too far to the right for them.

Our children will today attempt to repeat a story: It is the story of Jesus' birth, death, and resurrection. That I am sure you have heard hundreds of times in different ways, by different people with different meanings, but today you will hear it from the children of Bethel A.M.E. Church, New Bedford. Please bear with us because some of our children are telling this story for their first time. Hearing is a distinctly different verb from telling. The two are co-related, but different.

NOTES

Chapter 27
APRIL 14, 1977

Exert from a sermon preached at New England Annual Conference by Rev. Donald Luster:

Scripture: St. Luke 4:18
Theme: The Holy Spirit Speaks to the Church
Subject: God in His Contemporary Nativity

In Genesis the Spirit of God walks upon the water. The Hebrew concept of Yahweh: The Holy Spirit comes suddenly and unexpectedly upon individual people. Rua is the Hebrew word for Spirit. The Holy Spirit came upon Gideon and caused him to blow the trumpet. He became an instant leader. In the New Testament, Jesus was baptized by John the Baptist, the heavens open up and the Spirit from God came down like a dove. The Holy Spirit is Jesus revealing Himself in his own particular situation invisible, but belief in Jesus. The Holy Spirit is external symbol of Jesus. He tells all the teachings of Jesus Christ. God is three-in-one. There is no basic Christian doctrine more baffling than John 14. The disciples were performing choice of fellowship. Jesus tells the disciples 'do not worry, he will send them a comforter and leader, so that they will not be lost. This comforter will be the Holy Spirit. He will remind them of teachings. The Holy Spirit cannot be detected from Jesus Christ. They are one and the same. Growing revelation –we must have Christ in our heart. The Holy Spirit knows the future, but we weren't humble enough for the Spirit to reveal these things to us. God has a plan. It is His plan, not ours. Expose yourself to these things that suggest Jesus so as to receive the Holy Spirit. Go to church. Keep Jesus in chambers of your imagination. Abide in his words and let His words abide in you. Yearn highly to serve Him. The Holy Spirit is a coach when we have received Him, we become tools.

On the 15th, Rev. Luster continued with a seminar on the 'Holy Ghost.'

These are some of the highlights from that seminar:

The Holy Spirit is an agent from God and is God himself. The Holy Spirit tells us to do good things. It is a productive spirit. People who come will be benefactors. The Holy Ghost reflects and influences us differently. Open mind goes a long way with the Holy Ghost. Religious people are influenced by things of the world. Our perspectives have to be Christ centered as Christians. People express the presence of the Holy Ghost in different ways: minds and eyes focus on one thing, no sidetracks. The Holy Ghost/Holy Spirit-buoying about change in individual in whole atmosphere: Teacher, comforter, deliverer, guide, leader, director. The Holy Spirit is binding agent keeping us together. Of our own nature, we are doomed to destroy. The Holy Spirit has personality and is equipped with intelligence, self-determination. God is very essence of the Holy Spirit. The Holy Spirit is a mystery, but we know it is of God. He has three distinctive personalities with the same essence.

The Holy Spirit intercedes for you. Makes you feel guilty, feel undone. The Holy Spirit abides in you and never leaves.

These lessons came at a season in my life when I needed it most. God provided this opportunity and I cherish and treasure it.

Chapter 28
LETTER TO MAMA

My Dearest Mother,

This is Christmas Eve 1977, and the day is still bright. There is still a gleam of the sun. This brings to mind some Christmases I spent at home with you. At this very time of the day, we would all be sitting outside looking anxiously and waiting patiently for you. Once in a while there would be the sound of a firecracker in the neighborhood and if we did not have one to reply, we would be sad. It's only since becoming a Christian, I realize that every day is new and therefore so is Christmas. I can remember us raising cane on the veranda, some would be singing, "Christmas Come but once a year, we call it holiday." (Not knowing that this was line from slavery when that is the only day that slaves were not required to be in the cane field) One would start and then all would chime in and then the whole neighborhood would be singing that song. I can remember very well all the good times. We had a ball. Not everybody got a new dress, not everyone had shoes, but we enjoyed ourselves somehow.

We sat there and waited and waited and you would finally arrive. You were our Santa. We knew no other. We would all rush to meet you. Poor you! We would almost pull you down off the donkey or tear your clothes off of you. Mother, you are blessed as I am right now. I know I don't have the patience to go through all that. You would be so tired, but you had time to listen to all of us. You even stayed up with us midnight to give us the firecrackers and balloons. At the set of dawn, we would just be going to bed and at sunrise up again. What was so beautiful in those days, the children today would call them poverty. I miss most of all is that beautiful wind. Remember we used to have windmills decorated with annatto? Everybody had one. Sometimes, long after Christmas, they were hung up on the roof to catch the wind. Those days shall never return, mother. But I thank God for them and thank Him most of all for you. As I sit here and ponder and watch Gregory waiting anxiously for the next day, I cannot help feeling sorry for him because of the beautiful thing he has missed, and I will never be able to show it to him because out there have also changed so much.

Chapter 29
IN MY SORROW I CRIED OUT TO THE LORD

Must Jesus bear the cross alone? My telephone bugged. The doctors don't believe me. The police don't believe. My lawyer, whom I paid, did not believe me. But my Jesus, He saw my need and He walked with me and talked with me all the way. He did not leave me to carry these burdens alone. They were many and still are. He gave me strength to endure and courage to go on. There were many days when I did not think that I could live to see the morning, but one thing I was sure of, I would see my Jesus always.

What doubts, what fears, what anguish, sorrow, disillusionment? Lord, you and you alone could help me through. Through it all, I learnt to lean on Jesus more and more. I learnt to trust in Him. I learnt to call upon His name, morning, noon and night. I trusted in God and God alone. He certainly believed me. My Lord heard my cry of anguish and He answered me. He promised never to leave me alone and I can truly testify that He did not. When the entire world forsakes me, I know that Jesus still cares. I was expected to leave town, to be insane, but Jesus made the difference in my life. Come by here, Lord, come by here. Come by here, Lord, come by here. Somebody needs you, Lord, come by here.

Stricken? It was very easy to see God. It was very easy to see Christ, the baby in us and to feel him in us. I could feel an interpersonal relationship. I could very easily identify myself with him. To me, He was real and still is. On Christmas day, I could still look over the ocean and see as far as the horizon, the sun shone, and there was mama and papa and brothers and sisters and lots of friends. We all felt free on that day from the regular rounds and that was plenty. We even had a choice: who wants to stay home and who wants to go to the fair. But you know what? I chose to stay home.

Notes

Chapter 30

A Second Chance

August 9, 1980

This was a time of transition for me. After five years I started dating. Greg, my fourteen-year-old son did not like the idea. He had witnessed some of the abuse I suffered in my previous relationship and was afraid that this would be a repeat. We had discussion. He would have to report to his father on every move I make, and he feared that more than anything else. His father, my ex-husband, thought there was a chance of our getting back together. However, in my book, there was no chance of that happening. I was ready to move on.

O God, if only Gregory would shape up and be the kind of son that I really wish him to be. At this time, he has me torn between hate and love. Why should he behave in the manner he does? Maybe he feels the same way that I am feeling, but does not know how fully to express it, except by being stubborn and quiet. If only he would converse with me more freely. I had to interrupt my thoughts to call him. He sounded okay, maybe happy. I think that he realized that I must have a life of my own. Is it proper for a child to scold his parent? I love him very much and do not want to lose him, neither allows him to fail. I cannot bear to think that this relationship may have an adverse effect on him. I had hoped it would do him good and no harm at all, but because of outside influences it is doing him harm. Dear Lord, help him to learn that people must form relationships and only God has the authority to say whether it is right or wrong.

In stressful times in my life, I turn to singing of songs and hymns. Most of them I learnt from my mother. She had a habit of walking around the house singing and crying. And so, I have copied her. Here are four of those songs that carried me through:

Father, I stretch my hands to thee, no other help I know, if thou withdraw thyself from me, oh whither shall I go (Charles Wesley)?

Have thine own way, Lord. Have thine own way. Thou art the potter; I am the clay; mold me and make me after thy will, while I am waiting, yielded and still (Adelaide A. Pollard).

Like a ship that's tossed and driven
Battered by an angry sea
When the storms of life are raging
And their fury falls on

I looked up and wonder why this race is so hard to run
Then I say to myself,
Don't worry, the Lord will make a way somehow
(Hezekiah Walker).

Lead me, oh Lord, lead me
Lead me, guide me along the way
For if you lead me, I cannot stray
Lord, let me walk each day with thee
Lead me, oh Lord, lead me (Doris Akers).

I don't want to lose track of the Lord, no matter how evil things become and even the thought of it seems as if I am lost. I still want to hang on to God's unchanging hand. But still, I long to be perfectly whole I want to be washed whiter than snow. (James Nicholson).

The Lord has never failed me yet, and he has never failed anyone else either, so I will trust him till I die.

Chapter 31

The Departure of My Dear Sister

September 9, 1980

My dearest sister, Delores Victoria Watson Robinson, passed away tragically and suddenly today. She shall be greatly missed. The leader of the family! I shall never forget her and the kindness she has done for me and to me. I am praying that the Lord will give me the strength and courage and grace to carry on. We had so many things planned to do, but there is so much that we could have done together. May her soul rest in peace! Please Lord, I am hoping that even in her very last moments she had a word with You. I hope to see her someday by the banks of Jordan. She is the first to do many things, not even the least, death. So, I hope we will be ready. A born leader she is. She captured the hearts and minds of almost everyone with whom she came in touch.

Some come, some mourn, some were curious, others were numb or dumbfounded. Some came. For what reason, they do not know.

Some came to show
Some came to know
Some came to see
Some came to be seen
Whatever the reason
They were all welcomed
Everyone expressed their sympathy
In their own way
Some may cry
Others may laugh
Some may look steadfast and stare

Some may want to hate her
Even though she is dead
The love she gave
The gifts she presented
Will not ever be repaid
She did not give to receive
She gave so that someone would be happy
So that she herself could derive some joy from life
If she did not give, she was not happy.
Even in death, she gave herself.

The first born of our mother
And also, the first to return to the Father
This is the way Sister Del would like it to be
She, the leader and first to go and taste and see
And pave the way for us to follow.
My sister has left behind an invaluable legacy
No price high enough to place on it.
It cannot be auctioned
Neither bought nor sold
That legacy only can be revered and honored
And followed and continued.
Is my family ready to keep that legacy?
Active and alive!
Who will be the leader? Who will be Dell?
How many years will it take to produce another Dell?

Chapter 32

What They Say About God:

John 11:25, 26:

"Jesus said to her, 'I am the resurrection and the life. He who believes in me will live, even though he dies; and whoever lives and believes in me will never die.'"

They say God is infinite. Therefore, since God is life and love, life and love are infinite. If not love, life definitely is. But love, once it has been perceived and given, it cannot be taken back. It may change or discontinued but that same love, like a note in a song, once it has hit its peak, cannot be retracted. The memory of that love lives in your experience, in your life, whether good, bad, or indifferent. Life, in order for death or decay to take place, life must be present in some form. Death and decay are changed forms of life. There is no life; there is no room for decay. Decay itself is a life process. A degenerating cycle which when completed produces another simpler or more diversified form of life. Our bodies are continually decaying. Without decay, growth is stunned since there is no room for new and stronger layers. The aging process in human beings and animals and even trees or any living thing starts where growth stops.

Our pots and pans do not grow, but with the influence of the growing process around them, they also experience the aging process. This infinite God-given growth in life cannot be hindered by human beings. God has a plan for all living things whether or not it has a soul. Does this mean then that there is no death? I am inclined to define death as a change in life.

A leaf falls to the ground, decays, and forms the richest soil of all, humus. For decay to take place, life must be present at all times. The humus thus formed is also full of life: Life which supports strong, rich, growing plants and vegetables.

It is said that we cannot see death, only feel it. Life is not always full of vigor for all of us. From experience, I have learnt that in order to gain one must lose. In gambling, one must risk money or chances before even conceiving of winning.

Life is death and death is life. The two go hand in hand. After one dies, decay or corruption takes place, no matter what the circumstances is that cause death. There are people who asked that their bodies be cremated after death in order to avoid corruption. But what stands in the ashes that are produced, what has more life to it than ashes? If someone is swallowed by a layer more ferocious species of the animal kingdom, what becomes of the devoured body? It cannot be digested whole. It must decay within the primates' intestines in order for it to be digested. As a matter of fact, nothing can be digested whole. It must at all times be broken down either inside or outside the digestive tract of the mammal. Most plant life will rise up bigger and stronger after propagation. We must die to live. Just as the fetuses in our mother's womb.

To live is to die. To die is to live.

Chapter 33

September 20, 1980

These are thoughts following the tragic death and funeral of my sister:

As I sit here and watch the beautiful sun set, all the different colors and shades of colors. Colors too numerous to name, I begin to think of the life of Delores, my beloved sister, who has gone to eternal rest. The many different paths she had paved and had yet to pave. I come to the conclusion that man, just for the mere fact that he is in flesh and blood which equals corruption, is incomplete. Whatever is complete is perfect. What upon the face of the earth is perfect? We see perfect sunshine, perfect moonshine, done in the manner that only God Himself could do. We marvel at the secret beauty of the ocean. We look at a newborn baby and say, "How great is God and mighty are His works."

As we plan, the chart we map, we work and we aim for higher heights and deeper depth, but when do we know that we have reached? Jesus Christ hung on the cross; he said it is finished and gave up the ghost. What is finished? Not life. Not death. Not hope. Not love and loving. This particular mission is completed. The battle has been won. The victory is His.

A note of encouragement to my mother:

Dearest mother:

If only I had the talent and the gift to express to you how I truly feel. The most I can do is pray that God will give us grace and courage to carry on. Delores would not want us to stand up with arms folded. She would not want us to have long and sad faces. I am sure if she had the chance to say Goodbye to us, she would have said something like this: "Complete what I have started"; "Take care of mama and papa"; "Go to school and study hard"; "Take care of yourself"; "Continue to serve the Lord"; and "Please take care of my little Jean." We were all her children as far as she is concerned.

Chapter 34

ANOTHER CHRISTMAS, DECEMBER 25, 2007

Man, God, and Nature

Sitting on the porch at 6:00 a.m. looking out over the hills and into the ocean wide, glittering and blue and white just as the sky, I feel like God has shown me great delight. He has not hidden from me the beauty of His nature. I hear many sounds. I can't identify them. They are sounds of the creatures He himself created. It is musical, mystical, cheery, and rapturous. In time with God's own raw untouched scenery, I can't help feeling a great connection to Him. The wonders and beauty of the world are unfolding right before my eyes. Thank you, Lord.

Then I consider what if God had taken away my vision, how would I be able to see the relationship between the sky and the sea. The vastness of them! Thinking of creation, he drew boundaries between the earth and the sky and the sea. He did not command not to relate. They each serve their own purpose.

Look at all the birds flying around and frolicking. I hear the sounds of pigs and goats and dogs barking. Those are very distinct. However, those flying, frolicking creatures I cannot identify. They delude me and my hearing. Maybe one day I'll purchase a piece of equipment to help identify them. They sing solos and choruses. The thrilling can only be heard early in the morning. Wings are flopping fluttering. All indicate life. The trees support life. Not death.

I imagine they see the trees as their refuge—their God. After all, in them they find refuge and protection. There is food and shelter from the storms. They blend in with the colors to escape from the enemies, just like soldiers in combat. They know when to sing out loud and when to be silent. They know when to call out to each other. They are a community. They checkup on each other. They make a certain sound to alert others of enemy invasion. They are distinctly different, yet the same. Thank you, Lord for our differences and commonalities. They are the way you made us. There is a light refreshing cool breeze.

Chapter 35

Women Drivers Are Not Respected

While in Jamaica, I was taking one of my nieces to the hospital with her baby, I drove through a pothole and had a flat tire.

The street/highway is filled with major potholes. They are called potholes; however, they are more like sink holes. Their edges are razor sharp. They cause major damage to autos and delays too. For example, I was on my way to the hospital with a sick child, was she overactive, it would have been a great stress on the child and family. Surrounded by about fifteen others including my niece and grand-niece- and nephew-in-law, there is an extensive religious, theological, philosophical conversation going on about God, religion and church. Sounds like one is a practicing Seventh Day Adventist member! There is hardly any boundary between state and religion and the Seventh Day Adventists are the most popular.

The highways are used predominantly by men. The men are hostile to female drivers. They bad-drive the women! They will do road rage and outrageous actions which could possibly cause accidents. Female drivers must be bold, courageous, and unafraid. It is an area of the society which requires serious attention to correct grievous flaw in the society. Staying on the road and remaining focused and alert is a greater task than driving itself. The potholes and the male drivers are the challenges the women must face. Both are at times overpowering and could at times be overwhelming and frustrating. Both pose hazards to safety and security and the law enforcement officers should be aware of it. Or they are and choose to ignore the signs. Or they are part of the problem and not the solution.

There should be public outcry about it. It is not a women's issue. It affects all people, driver and pedestrians, male and female. Everyone needs to speak out against this form of harassment and gender discrimination. The men are like hogs on the road. They must be told that taxes are paid by both men and women. In spite of all that stress, women are forging ahead.

Chapter 36

WORDS OF ENCOURAGEMENT

Bible verses:

Psalm 46:1(NIV)	God is our refuge and strength, an ever-present help in trouble.
Proverbs 18:10 (NIV)	The name of the Lord is a strong tower, the righteous run to it and are safe.
Nehemiah 8:10b (NIV)	Do not grieve, for the joy of the Lord is your strength.

- Find yourself
- Cheer up and live life
- Each time the memory surfaces prepare to deal with it
- You have to fight through some bad days to earn the best days of your life
- Who can help you?
- Make time to help others
- You will become a better person
- Trouble don't last always
- Talk to someone
- Challenges only come to make you strong
- Pick yourself up and keep moving
- Choose the people surrounding you
- Are "friends" real friends?
- You have a choice: give in, give up, or give it all you've got

- Accept and acknowledge your weakness, in so doing you will be strong
- What have you learned from the experience?
- What can you share with others?
- Seek professional therapy
- Stick with the positive things of the past
- Attend church
- Read the Bible
- Go to work
- Improve your educational level: attend college

BIBLIOGRAPHY

Akers, Doris. Lead me, O Lord, lead me: African Methodist Episcopal Hymnal, pg. 378

Pollard, Adelaide A. Have Thine Own Way Lord: African Methodist Episcopal Church Hymnal, pg. 345

Tom Wolfe: O Rotten Gotham essay

Walker, Hezekiah. Like a Ship That's Tossed and Driven.

Wesley, Charles. Father I Stretch My hands To Thee: African Methodist Episcopal Church Hymnal, pg. 317

NOTES

ABOUT THE AUTHOR

Birdilyn was born in Jamaica, West Indies, in the parish of St. Elizabeth, to Luther and Myrtle Watson. She is the twelfth of fifteen children. When she was five years old, the family moved to Peters Ville, Westmoreland, where most of her family in Jamaica still resides.

Her first five years of education was in the Kings Elementary School. She completed her elementary education at Gordon Town Government School in St. Andrew, then moved on to Above Rocks High School in St. Catherine, and finally matriculated from Alpha Academy in Kingston in 1965. In April 1968, Birdilyn migrated to the United States.

Since coming to the United States, Birdilyn has earned her Master's in Management and Counseling from Cambridge College and a Bachelor of Science in Management from University of Massachusetts Dartmouth. She is an ordained local elder in the African Methodist Episcopal Church.

Birdilyn volunteered for many years on the rape crisis hot-line at the Women's Center and also as a member on the Board of Directors where she worked to have lawmakers and law enforcement officers recognize the impact of domestic violence on the individual, the home, and the community. She was also a member of the Board of Directors of the Young Women Christian Association and the Interchurch Counsel of Greater New Bedford. Another organization of which Birdilyn has been a member and officer of is the Church Women United.

Birdilyn is the mother of two biological children, nine stepchildren, and twenty-six grandchildren. Reading, writing, spending time with her family, and preaching keeps her busy. She is now retired from the New Bedford Public School, where she worked as a guidance counselor, and from Commonwealth Gas and Electric Company, where she worked as a customer service representative. She spends most of the winter in Jamaica.